W9-AYF-557

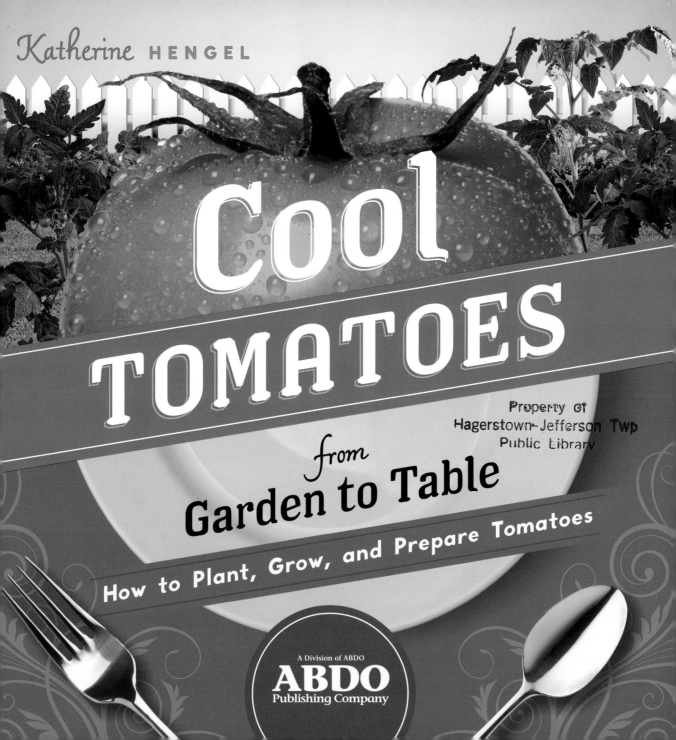

Katherine HENGEL

Cool
TOMATOES

from
Garden to Table

How to Plant, Grow, and Prepare Tomatoes

A Division of ABDO
ABDO
Publishing Company

visit us at www.abdopublishing.com

Published by ABDO Publishing Company, a division of ABDO, P.O. Box 398166, Minneapolis, Minnesota 55439. Copyright © 2012 by Abdo Consulting Group, Inc. International copyrights reserved in all countries. No part of this book may be reproduced in any form without written permission from the publisher. Checkerboard Library™ is a trademark and logo of ABDO Publishing Company.

Printed in the United States of America, North Mankato, Minnesota
102011
012012

 PRINTED ON RECYCLED PAPER

Design and Production: Anders Hanson, Mighty Media, Inc.
Series Editor: Liz Salzmann
Photo Credits: Aaron DeYoe, Shutterstock. Photos on page 5 courtesy of W. Atlee Burpee & Co.

The following manufacturers/names appearing in this book are trademarks: Argo®, Barilla®, Hellmann's®, Heinz®, Market Pantry®, Galbani®, Crystal Sugar®, Pyrex®, E-Z Foil®, Kitchen Aid®, Chefmate®

Library of Congress Cataloging-in-Publication Data
Hengel, Katherine.
 Cool tomatoes from garden to table : how to plant, grow, and prepare tomatoes / Katherine Hengel.
    p. cm. -- (Cool garden to table)
 Includes index.
 ISBN 978-1-61783-187-4
 1. Tomatoes--Juvenile literature. 2. Cooking (Tomatoes)--Juvenile literature. I. Title.
 SB349.H365 2012
 635'.642--dc23
                    2011037819

Safety First!
Some recipes call for activities or ingredients that require caution. If you see these symbols, ask an adult for help!

Sharp - *You need to use a sharp knife or cutting tool for this recipe.*

Hot - *This recipe requires handling hot objects. Always use oven mitts when holding hot pans.*

CONTENTS

WHY GROW YOUR OWN FOOD?

Because then you get to eat it, of course! You might not be the biggest tomato fan in the world. But have you ever had fresh tomatoes? Straight from your very own garden? If not, prepare to be surprised. Fresh food tastes wonderful!

Plus, fresh food is really healthy. All produce is good for you. But produce that comes from your own garden is the very best. Most folks do not use chemicals in their home gardens. That makes home gardens better for you and the **environment**!

Growing your own food is rewarding. All it takes is time, patience, soil, water, and sunshine! This book will teach you how to grow patio tomatoes. Once they're ready, you can use them in some tasty recipes!

TOMATOES

There are more than 7,000 kinds of tomatoes. Each looks, tastes, and grows differently. Most tomatoes are red. But some are yellow, orange, purple, green, or even white. They come in different shapes and sizes too.

Many tomatoes were created to grow well on patios. The plants don't get too big, but they produce a lot of tomatoes!

Cherry tomatoes are a popular patio tomato. But the recipes in this book work best with bigger tomatoes. So pick your favorite mid-size patio tomato, and let's get started!

TYPES OF TOMATOES

| CHERRY | BEEFSTEAK | EARLY GIRL | BRANDYWINE HEIRLOOM | ROMA |

GROWING

In this book, you'll learn how to grow tomatoes in a **container** garden. With container gardens, you have more control over things such as light and temperature. But keep in mind that tomatoes grow differently in every climate.

When to Plant

Go online to find out the average date of the last frost in your area. Plant your **seedling** about one week after this date.

The Right Conditions

Sunlight
Tomato plants need six to eight hours of sunlight a day.

Temperature
Tomatoes like the daytime temperature to be between 70 and 80 degrees. If it gets too cold, bring your tomato plants inside.

Pests and Weeds
Be earth-friendly! Soap and water sprays keep pests away. White vinegar is a great weed killer.

Shade
Put your container in a location that gets some natural shade. Or bring it inside if it gets too hot.

The Right Soil
Fertile, well-draining soil is a must! Also, make sure there is plenty of nitrogen in the soil when you plant your seedling.

PLANT YOUR

SEEDLING

1

2

3

MATERIALS NEEDED

5 gallon container with drainage holes

soil

tomato seedling

tomato stake

mulch

water

trowel

(1) Fill your **container** three-quarters full of soil. Break up the soil so it is loose. Make a hole in the center.

(2) Carefully remove the **seedling** from its container. Set it in the hole. Arrange the soil around the plant so it is supported.

(3) You may need to stake your plant. Put the stake in the soil near the seedling. Make sure the bottom of the stake hits the bottom of the container.

4 Add **mulch** around the seedling. Then water the plant thoroughly.

STAGES OF

Watering

The trick is to water tomatoes heavily but not too often. Let the soil dry out between each watering. Always water your plants in the morning. Direct the water at the base of the plant. Try not to get the leaves wet.

Mulching

Using **mulch** will lock in moisture. It also keeps water and soil from splashing up onto the leaves.

WATER your plant when the soil is dry. Try to avoid getting water on the leaves.

MULCH your seedling right after planting it.

FERTILIZE every 10 days at first. Then every two weeks while the plant is blooming. Don't fertilize after tomatoes start to appear.

GROWTH

Fertilizing

Tomato plants should be **fertilized** every 10 days until they start blooming. Feed them every two weeks while they are blooming. Stop fertilizing when tomatoes start to form.

Staking & Pruning

If you are growing a staked tomato, you will need to tie it to the stake. Do this when the plant starts to fall over. Remove lower leaves when the plant is small. After that, remove any new stems that start growing. This helps the main stem grow better.

STAKE your plant if it starts to fall over. Tie it to the stake with string or cloth.

HARVEST when the tomatoes reach their full color and are soft to the touch.

HARVESTING

TOMATOES

1. Pick tomatoes when they reach their full color and are soft to the touch.

2. Wash and dry the tomatoes. They'll keep at room temperature for about a week. Store them in the refrigerator if you're not going to use them right away. Or learn how to can them!

3. Tomatoes can't ripen when the temperature is below 60 **degrees**. Bring the green tomatoes inside. Store them in a brown paper bag. The warmth in the bag will cause the tomatoes to ripen.

Tomato Q & A

QUESTIONS

& ANSWERS

How Long Will it Take?

It depends on the sun, temperature, and type of tomato. Generally, **seedlings** need 60 to 90 days to grow ripe tomatoes.

Why are there black spots on my leaves? Or on my tomatoes?

These spots can be caused by several kinds of **fungi** and bacteria. Remove the **infected** leaves. If there are spots on a tomato, throw it away.

Why did my tomatoes split?

Changes in the weather or water supply can cause cracks in the tomatoes. Cracks are like stretch marks. The tomato grew too fast in too short of time.

Why is there a big black spot around the stem of my tomato?

This is caused by a lack of **calcium**. This happens when it doesn't get enough water. Plants **absorb** calcium along with water from the soil through their roots. If they don't get water, they can't get calcium.

Cool Ingredients

9-INCH UNCOOKED PIE SHELL

BAGUETTE

CORNSTARCH

FETTUCCINE

FRESH BASIL

FRESH CILANTRO

GARLIC CLOVES

GRATED CHEDDAR CHEESE

GREEN ONIONS

HONEY

LEMON JUICE

MARJORAM

DID YOU KNOW?

Tomatoes are actually a fruit. But they are usually cooked and eaten more like vegetables.

MAYONNAISE

OLIVE OIL

RED ONION

ORANGE JUICE

PARMESAN CHEESE

RED WINE VINEGAR

REGULAR AND FRESH MOZZARELLA

SALT & PEPPER

SOURDOUGH BREAD

SUGAR

Kitchen Tools

BAKING SHEET

BASTING BRUSH

BREAD KNIFE

CUTTING BOARD

GRATER

KITCHEN SCISSORS

LARGE POT

MEASURING CUPS

MEASURING SPOONS

MIXING BOWLS

MIXING SPOON

OVEN MITTS

Before slicing or chopping tomatoes, ask an adult to sharpen the knife for you. It's important to use a sharp knife when cutting tomatoes.

PAPER TOWELS

PASTA SERVER

PIE PAN

PLASTIC WRAP

PLATE

POT HOLDERS

SHARP KNIFE

SPATULA

SPOON

STRAINER

WHISK

Cooking Terms

Arrange

Arrange means to place things in a certain order or pattern.

Brush

Brush means to spread a liquid on something using a basting brush.

Chop

Chop means to cut into small pieces.

Drain

Drain means to remove liquid using a strainer or colander.

Drizzle

Drizzle means to slowly pour a liquid over something.

Grate

Grate means to shred something into small pieces using a grater.

Slice

Slice means to cut food into pieces of the same thickness.

Spread

Spread means to make a smooth layer with a spoon, knife, or spatula.

Toss

Toss means to turn ingredients over to coat them with seasonings.

Whisk

Whisk means to beat quickly by hand with a whisk or a fork.

Orange Salsa

Kiss your old salsa recipe good-bye!

MAKES 2½ CUPS

INGREDIENTS

3 medium-sized tomatoes

½ medium-sized red onion

¼ cup fresh cilantro

1 tablespoon orange juice

1 teaspoon sugar

1 teaspoon salt

TOOLS

sharp knife

cutting board

measuring cups

medium mixing bowl

measuring spoons

mixing spoon

plastic wrap

(1) Cut off the top and bottom of a tomato. Set the tomato on the cutting board. Place the tip of the knife in the center of the top of the tomato and cut down.

(2) Gently pull the tomato open and set it down on the cutting board. Use the knife to cut away the insides of the tomato.

3 Repeat steps 1 and 2 with the other tomatoes.

(4) Chop the tomato skins and red onion into small pieces. Finely chop the cilantro. Put the tomatoes, onions, and cilantro in a medium bowl.

(5) Add the orange juice, sugar, and salt. Mix well. Cover the bowl with plastic wrap. Chill the salsa for 1 hour before serving.

Tomato Salad

Cheese and tomatoes come together for a refreshing meal!

INGREDIENTS

1 pound assorted tomatoes

6 to 7 slices fresh mozzarella cheese

1 teaspoon salt

1½ tablespoon red wine vinegar

½ teaspoon honey

¼ cup olive oil

2 sprigs marjoram

5 to 7 fresh basil leaves

TOOLS

sharp knife

cutting board

kitchen scissors

measuring spoons

medium mixing bowl

whisk

measuring cups

plate

spoon

① Slice the large tomatoes. Leave the smaller tomatoes whole, or cut them in half. Arrange the tomato and cheese slices on a plate.

② Put the the salt, vinegar, and honey in a medium bowl. Whisk until the salt **dissolves**. Then whisk in the olive oil. Drizzle the dressing over the tomatoes and mozzarella.

③ Strip the marjoram leaves from the stems. Add them to the salad. Use kitchen scissors cut up the basil leaves. Sprinkle the pieces over the salad. Add salt to taste.

1

2

3

CRISPY
Caprese Melt

Your favorite salad is now a sandwich!

MAKES 1 SANDWICH

INGREDIENTS

2 slices sourdough bread

½ tablespoon olive oil

6 fresh basil leaves

1 medium-sized tomato, sliced ¼ inch thick

1 ounce fresh mozzarella cheese, sliced ¼ inch thick

salt and pepper

TOOLS

cutting board

sharp knife

measuring spoons

basting brush

baking sheet

oven mitts

spatula

(1) **Adjust** an oven rack so it is six inches from the top. Set the oven to broil. Brush one side of a bread slice with olive oil. Place it oil side down on a baking sheet.

(2) Arrange the basil leaves, tomato slices, and mozzarella slices on the bread. Sprinkle lightly with salt and pepper.

(3) Put the other bread slice on top. Brush it with olive oil. Broil the **sandwich** for 1 minute. Remove it from the oven. Turn the sandwich over with a spatula.

(4) Put it back in the oven. Broil for 1 to 2 more minutes. The bread should be golden brown, and the cheese should be slightly melted. Slice the sandwich in half and serve immediately.

1

2

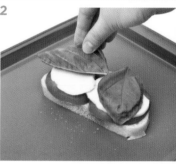

3

4

FRESH
Tomato Pasta

Enjoy the contrast of cool tomatoes and warm pasta!

MAKES 4 TO 6 SERVINGS

INGREDIENTS

1 pound fettuccine pasta

4 to 6 tomatoes, chopped

5 tablespoons olive oil

2 teaspoons lemon juice

⅓ cup fresh basil, chopped

salt and pepper

½ cup grated Parmesan cheese

TOOLS

large pot

measuring spoons

measuring cups

cutting board

sharp knife

large mixing bowl

mixing spoon

strainer

pasta server

pot holders

① Cook the fettuccine according to the instructions on the package.

② Put the tomatoes, olive oil, lemon juice, and basil in a large bowl. Add salt and pepper to taste. Mix gently.

③ Drain the pasta when it is done. Put it in the bowl with the tomato mixture. Toss to mix. Sprinkle the Parmesan cheese on top. Serve immediately.

To Taste?

Sometimes a recipe says to add an ingredient "to taste." That means you decide how much to add! Start small. You can always add more later. It's harder to remove something than it is to add more!

1

2

3

BRILLIANT
Bruschetta

This simple, satisfying appetizer will go fast!

MAKES 12 PIECES

INGREDIENTS

12 baguette slices,
½ inch thick

olive oil

salt

3 to 4 medium tomatoes,
finely chopped

2 teaspoons finely
chopped fresh basil

pepper

1 garlic clove, halved

½ cup grated
mozzarella cheese

TOOLS

cutting board

bread knife

measuring cups

basting brush

baking sheet

measuring spoons

mixing bowl

mixing spoon

oven mitts

sharp knife

1. Set the oven to broil. Brush both sides of each piece of bread with olive oil. Put the bread slices on a baking sheet. Sprinkle them lightly with salt.

2. Mix the tomatoes, basil, and 2 tablespoons of olive oil in a bowl. Add salt and pepper to taste. Set the bowl aside.

3. Broil the bread for about 2 minutes. Turn the slices over. Broil for 2 more minutes. Watch the bread carefully. It should be browned but still soft in the center. Remove the bread from the oven. Let it cool slightly. Rub the halved garlic clove on each slice.

4. Put some of the tomato mixture on each bread slice. Add some mozzarella cheese to each piece. Put the baking sheet back in the oven for 1 minute. Then serve it immediately.

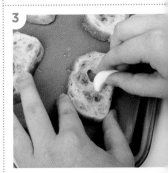

TOMATO
Pie in the Sky

Only garden fresh tomatoes will do!

MAKES 1 PIE

INGREDIENTS

4 medium-sized
tomatoes, sliced

salt

9-inch uncooked
pie shell

½ cup plus
3 tablespoons grated
Parmesan cheese

½ cup chopped
green onion

¾ cup mayonnaise

1½ cups grated
cheddar cheese

2 teaspoons cornstarch

¼ cup chopped fresh
basil leaves

pepper

TOOLS

cutting board

sharp knife

paper towels

measuring cups

pie pan

measuring spoons

medium mixing bowl

mixing spoon

oven mitts

1. Preheat the oven to 375 **degrees**. Put the tomato slices on paper towels. Sprinkle them with salt. Let them stand 10 minutes.

2. Put the uncooked pie shell in a pie pan. Sprinkle it with 3 tablespoons Parmesan cheese. Arrange the tomatoes and green onions in the pie shell.

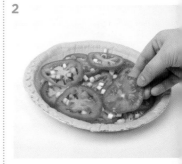

3. Put the mayonnaise, cheddar cheese, ⅓ cup Parmesan cheese, cornstarch, and basil in a medium mixing bowl. Add salt and pepper to taste. Mix well.

4. Gently place spoonfuls of the mayonnaise mixture on the tomatoes. Carefully spread the mixture over the pie.

5. Sprinkle the remaining Parmesan cheese over the top. Bake for 30 to 40 minutes. The pie crust and mayonnaise mixture should be golden brown.

WRAP IT UP!

Did you enjoy growing food from the earth? Are you a gifted cook with fresh ingredients? Fresh ingredients go a long way toward making food taste great. Ask the best chefs in the world. They'll tell you! Fresh ingredients are their secret ingredients!

By now you know that fresh food tastes great. Plus, it's good for the **environment**. Food from your garden doesn't require **transportation** or packaging. It isn't covered in harmful chemicals either!

So keep at it. Don't lose that green thumb! Think about your favorite foods. Can you grow them yourself? Chances are, you can. Check out the other books in this series. There may be a book about growing and cooking your favorite food!

Glossary

ABSORB – to soak up or take in.

ADJUST – to change something slightly.

CALCIUM – a soft, white element that most plants and animals need to be healthy.

CONTAINER – something that other things can be put into.

DEGREE – the unit used to measure temperature.

DISSOLVE – to mix with a liquid so that it becomes part of the liquid.

ENVIRONMENT – nature and everything in it, such as the land, sea, and air.

FERTILIZE – to add something to the soil to make plants grow better.

FUNGUS – an organism, such as mold or mildew, that grows on rotting plants. The plural of *fungus* is *fungi*.

INFECTED – to have a disease caused by bacteria or other germs.

MULCH – something, such as straw or wood chips, spread over the ground to protect plants.

NITROGEN – a gas that is in all living things and makes up most of the earth's atmosphere.

SANDWICH – two pieces of bread with a filling, such as meat, cheese, or peanut butter, between them.

SEEDLING – a young plant that grew from a seed.

TRANSPORTATION – the act of moving people and things.

Index